Fully Loaded

Evangelist Sandra Green

ISBN 978-1-63575-310-3 (Paperback)
ISBN 978-1-63575-311-0 (Digital)

Christian Faith Publishing, Inc.
296 Chestnut Street
Meadville, PA 16335
www.christianfaithpublishing.com

Printed in the United States of America

Contents

Introduction

This book gives me great joy because it is birthed out of trials, tribulations, storms, good times, and knowing who I am and what I am created for. It's a book that has been in my soul for a long time. It was in God's timing. He allowed me to go through with His strength and showed His amazing love in spite of my circumstance and where my faith was in those times. Sometimes we think we are ready, but God knows the timing when we are to fully and totally surrender to Him to be equipped for the journey ahead. He teaches us through our storms and shapes us for what He has purposed our lives to be. He wants to be glorified in us, so thank you, God, for your timing and not mine. Life has not always been rough. There were some good times as well as not-so-good times. I confess that if it had not been for the LORD on my side, I would not have seen the manifestation of this revelation of this book, *Fully Loaded*. I could give you details of many storms in my life, but this book cannot contain all of it. I pray with the leading and guidance of the Holy Spirit and God's Words from Heaven. I will share and testify of God's goodness, mercy, and strength He gave me to overcome and be at this point in my life to give back the treasures of His word and love to others to help them overcome in times of adversities and to point them in the direction of the cross. I can only say if you trust Him no matter what you are going through, He will see you through. Every chance the Lord allows me to share a word, I strive to be an encourager and use the blueprints of my storms to let someone else know you can make it if you stay fully loaded with the armor of God. The ingredients to staying fully loaded are in the Word of God. We all have a purpose in this life. First, we must recognize the meaning of our lives. That we are wonderfully and fearfully made by Him. It is a gift from God. You must have a clear sense of your purpose in life. I went through a phase in my life where I questioned my purpose to be here. Because of circumstances and things we face today, we seem to beat ourselves up getting an answer and the only one with the answer is God. To understand our purpose, we have to understand God. We must have a relationship with God. I found that the only way I could get the answer is to have a relationship with God, and I discovered I have access to Him, and I can ask Him and read His Word to know my purpose, and I did. But before getting to that answer, my life endured some spiritual warfares that left scars. But praise God, those scars brought me out of the warfares in my life. I now recognize and admit that He is our strong tower. Knowing our purpose enables us to rise to life's challenges. God put something in each of us that is unique to accomplish what he created us for. I get my greatest breakthrough when I worship and praise Him in the midst of what I am going through. He prepares us for every battle we face and equips us to win the battles. Victory comes when we stay fully loaded with the Word of God and trust Him that everything in your life works for the good. I pray that you will be spiritually uplifted by this book by the words from God through the Spirit of God and the love He has for us that never changes no matter what we go through. You are a conqueror!

Turn Off the Noise in My Head

(Be Transformed by the Renewing of Your Mind)

Do not conform to the problem of this world, but be transformed by the renewing of your mind. (Romans 12:2)

Mentally we hear constant chatter in our minds every day, from the time we wake up and the moment we fall asleep. Often, the noise in my head keep me awake until you turn it off and connect in the Spirit by praying and asking God to help you turn off the noise of the world. Whether we are thinking of what we did yesterday, a song we heard, someone made us mad. Family member not acting right, negative past situation, or we may visualize something that happened in the past or present and can't seem to overcome it. Thinking of things we are going to do today and even tomorrow. Fear is the number one enemy that cripples our minds. We never seem to enjoy the moments when good things are happening. We seem to think that our minds cannot be transformed from thinking evil thoughts to good.

It's a war going on in our minds, and we can't seem to turn it off. In your inner thoughts, sometimes you are able to switch your thinking on and off at will. Many times I have spoken to myself and asserted myself that I was in control; after all, I told my mind to be still, and no sooner than I thought I was peaceful and in control, a noise distracted me. Mental noise is constant; it never stops. We converse with ourselves constantly. Paul said in Romans 7:19, "For the good that I would I do not: but the evil which I would not that I do." Oh, we may laugh at Paul, but we know that it's fundamentally true: we want to turn the noise off, and we know we should, but we don't. We know the results of not thinking the right thoughts, yet we yield to our minds not being transformed but conformed to the ways of the world. We need to quiet our mind. Be still.

I find my greatest victories were when my mind was aligned to God who has given us a blueprint of having a peace that surpasses all understanding. Inner peace. Philippians 4:7 says, "And the peace of God, which passeth all understanding, shall keep your hearts and minds through Christ Jesus." An inner calm will dominate your heart. I believe that many of our illnesses are due to the stressors we put on our bodies. I endured a storm in my life that brought me close to death's doors. God allowed me to make a decision for myself whether I wanted to turn off the noise of the enemy attacking my minds with things like "You are not going to get well. Why don't you just give up? Where is God if He says He loves you? Why is God making you suffer like this? After all, you read your Bible, you go to church. You feed the poor and help the sick." I had to turn off the noise and speak life to myself to bring a state of inner peace. This is a state that should be sought by all believers who wish to bring about peace and joy in their lives. There are moments we do experience inner peace without mental noise. It is something we need to practice and adopt as part of our everyday life, find activities that calm your inner man: meditation, fellowship, praying to God. When you find that inner calmness, hold on to it and practice it every day until it becomes a lifestyle. When we practice something long enough, you will be able to go back to that thing that brought you balance and peace and stability. Focus on things that bring peace.

We have to train our mind. The reason your mind keeps you in disarray is because you have trained it to be alert to negative things instead of the positive. Quieting our mind takes practice and determination. As Christians, we understand that we must mature on this journey. We must possess an awareness of where we are spiritually, be honest about your wars that are going on in your head. We all have struggles. None of our lives is so together that we don't have these struggles going on. Some of us don't want to admit them. This is not a sign of immaturity. I found that in my weakest moments of not trusting God, God showed Himself strong in me. He revealed Himself and diminished the thoughts in my mind that there was something wrong with me. His words to me are "Trust Me." Trust in the Lord with all your heart and do nor lean to your own understanding; in all your ways acknowledge Him, and He will direct your path (Proverbs 3:6). When we come into real acceptance of who we are and whose we are, we begin to defer our abilities to cope without Him. Paul wrote in Romans 8 of the power of the Holy Spirit, the power of the Holy Spirit that comes into your life and gives you strength. The Holy Spirit will help you do what is right.

You have the power through Christ to turn off the noise and allow your mind to empty itself of the negatives and fill it with positive thoughts with the help of the Holy Spirit.

Self-Worth

Knowing your self-worth, your outward manifestation of inner struggles. First, we must know who we are and identify our struggles and know who has the power to help us be overcomers and not prisoners of our emotions and thoughts. We are fearfully and wonderfully made by God (Psalm 139:14). We are handmade. Because of the love of God, He manifested Himself in the priceless display of His only-begotten Son Jesus's crucifixion and resurrection. While we were yet in sin, Jesus died (Romans 5:8). If we would take a moment to just digest that thought. Jesus died for you and me. He revealed Himself in the form of love (John 3:16). Ask yourself, "Who am I?" Then answer it with assurance that you know who you and whose you are. We have to free our minds from a victim mentality. A victim mentally is not letting go of things that keep you moving forward and people that keep you bound. Some may say it's easy to say let go. It is not easy in your will, but in God's will, we can do all things. The Word of God says there is only one sin that God will not forgive: blaspheming the Holy Spirit. All other sins are forgiven. This does not give us a free rein to sin because the Word says should we continue in sin God forbids, for the wages of sin is death and the gift of God is eternal live. We allow others to dictate our lives and give us their opinions on who they think we should be by what they see and how we interact in society. Some of us are good actors; we smile when really we are hurting, and we believe no one knows, but we should be assured that God sees and knows all things (Hebrews 4:13). He is omnipotent and omnipresent. He knows what we are thinking before we think it and even act on it. We have to connect our soul and mind together. The Word of God says, "So a man thinketh so is he." Life is in the tongue. If you don't know who you are, you will not function in this world. You will get by, but you will not enjoy the fullness of God. You will be tossed and driven by every wind that blows, by every negative word said to you, by opinion of others because you are not assured in yourself of your self-worth. Even when we mess up, God does not attack our self-worth; in fact, He gives us chances to get it right. He continues to assure us that He loves us and He proved it on the cross. Every day we rise if our mind-set is not in tune to who we are; we function as helpless individuals in this world, trying to find a place where we fit. God gave us gifts. Some of us have not open the gifts and use them to develop our character and enhance our well-being to move forward and own up to what God has created us to be; the purpose and journeys we will go through to get to our destiny. Where do I begin? First, ask yourself, "Who am I? What is my self-worth? I know I was just not created; I was created for something in God's Kingdom. The paintbrush is in God's hands, and the color selection is yours. If you chose black for the day because you feel down, ask God to lift you up out of that state of mind and color yourself yellow. "God, even though I feel dark and gloomy, by coloring me yellow, I see the rising of the sun and the going down of the same." You choose the color. You are the canvas, and the outcome of what's on the canvas is how God perceives you, not how you perceive yourself. We do not function properly when we have a defeated attitude; we don't feel loved; we feel tossed and driven. Our storms and trials have gotten the best of us because our faith is weak. There many things we are struggling to overcome; some have been damaged, but there is no sorrow heaven cannot feel. God showed us that Jesus's self-worth was not based on who He was, but it was based on what was inside of Him, Love that was willing to die for the sins of the world. Love, in spite of what happen in your life. He is there to help you stand tall, look up, tell yourself, "I am somebody"; I have a purpose; I will speak life to myself. I will make a difference because God will help me each day to trust and believe and pray and know

I am somebody. Practice, meditate and encourage yourself in the Lord. He is listening and ready to help you take back your rightful position in your heart and mind that you are a child of the most High God. You have to say, "How do I perceive myself?" You have to see yourself as competent. You have to constantly reinforce yourself every day. Focus on what you can do instead of what you cannot do. We have to focus on our strengths, not our weaknesses. Don't admit to something you can't do, then you think you are incompetent. Philippians 4:13 says, "I can do all things through Christ that strengthens me." Approach God with freedom and confidence. He loves you. There are other areas you are stronger in. So if you lack a particular skill, it does not make you incompetent. For our self-worth, we should know our accomplishments and our failures. It's a choice. Don't keep failing at something that is not your strength and recognize your abilities. He knows our weakness; He says when we are weak, He is strong! Set yourself free! God did! Galatians 5:1 gives us that assurance. John 8:36 gives us that assurance, "If the Son therefore will set you free, you will truly be the children of liberty." Christ, in the gospel, offer us freedom; he has power to do this, and those whom Christ makes free are." The Son is he who gives power to become the sons of God. Don't allow the enemy to entertain your mind that you have no self-worth; God never discredits our character. He always loves us despite how we feel about ourselves, and He is always looking for ways to show us every day that He loves us. That's priceless!

Failures Builds Character

For whatever is born of God overcomes the world. And this is the victory that has overcome the world, our faith. (Romans 3:23)

All of us have sinned and fallen short of God's glory. But God treats us much better than we deserve, and because of Christ Jesus, he freely accepts us and sets us free from sins. (1 John 5:4)

In our failures, the world beats us up, but God lifts us up, and He helps us correct ourselves in our failures. Does that mean we should dwell on our failures or repeat the same behaviors? No, the first thing is to acknowledge your mistakes, our shortcomings, and work to better ourselves through Christ. Speak positive things to yourself. Sometimes it means moving on to something else we can do better. Sometime it means giving ourselves more practice. You may say negative things to yourself like, "That was a horrible experience." Change it to "It was a challenging experience. It did not destroy me; it made me stronger."

"Can't do it" and "I give up"; change it to "I can do it and will give it my all."

"I am not good enough"; change it to "I am good enough and I am able."

"I can't stand that person"; change it to "Perhaps I am seeing something in that person that I see in myself."

"What's the use in trying again?" Change it to "I will keep trying till I get it right."

Whatever the situation, it's best to look for the advantages, gifts, and benefits gained than to dwell on one's real or imagined losses. Even losses or failures can become the motivation and fuel in future gains. Viewing something correctly means first changing the way in which you view it and thereafter think and speak about it. Try changing your language, and you will notice a profound difference in the way you feel, how you behave, and what you achieve.

Attitude is everything! Call your trials learning experiences or stepping-stones to the greater God has for your life. Some act as if their life's purpose is to prove they have been through something; we all have. We demonstrate our pain and loss by limiting the amount of joy, love, and prosperity that we should be enjoying. Talking endlessly about your victim story, losses, failures, and difficulties, we waste the power we have over our situation and spend precious energy and time in reinforcing the events of yesterday.

This doesn't mean you shouldn't fight back when you are actually victimized. Do what you need to do but without anger, resentment, or hate. Anger has a negative effect on the body, as well as the mind. Those who harbor anger or carry resentment for any length have defeated themselves.

Remember, you are already a success for you are a precious child of God. Jeremiah 8:4–5 says, "The Lord said: People of Jerusalem, when you stumble and fall, you get back up, and if you take a wrong road, you turn around and go back. So why do you refuse to come back to me? Why do you hold so tightly to your false God?"

If you keep looking back at your failures, you will never win the race that is set before you. To build your character from failures: (1) Run to God and ask Him, if you do not know. (2) Throw yourself at God's mercy. Ask His counsel. (3) Remember God's character, remember His promises Remember to fail from time to time is only human, but to be a "failure" is when we are defeated by failure, refusing to rise and try again. God has marked out a course for each of us, and sometimes that course includes failures. Remember we are more than conquerors. "No, in all things we are more than conquerors through him who loved us" (Romans 8:37).

The Right Position

Looking unto Jesus, the author and finisher of our faith, who for the joy that set before Him endured the cross—the shame—and is set down at the right hand—the throne of God. (Hebrews 12:2)

Position is very important in our walk with the Lord. It is not necessarily looking up in the natural form of man, but it is having our spirit and mind in the right position. In the human sense, we can stand and look up to the sky, but that does not mean we are in the right position. It means we are looking up and everyone around us view us with the position of our heads elevated, gazing in an upward position. If that was the only thing we were doing, it is just a position of looking up in the natural. What are we looking at? First, our heart and mind must be in agreement with why we took that position and what will be the outcome of our position.

We have been taught that the position to God is looking up. Looking up begins in the heart and mind. There is a commercial from Capital One, "What's in Your Wallet?" I ask, "What's in your heart?" In this spiritual walk with the Lord, it is important to be in position to be in alignment with the Lord.

We are under attack. For though we walk in the flesh, we do not war according to the flesh. For this fight we fight is not carnal; it's spiritual. So, we must be in the right position to win. I found out that every time I was out of position, the devil beat me mentally and physically up. When you are out of position, you are not much threat to Satan. Now you are distracted. It's all about you and what you are going through. So, I found out if I am not in alignment with God's Word, I lose. Here are some things that come under attack, the family. The modern family is no longer made up of a man, his wife, and their children ordained by God. Today's family need only be people living together for a given time. They can be single or even in relationship with someone of the same sex. We have accepted that as long as two people are loving each other, it's okay. Our adults have gotten out of position of being a role model for the children. Our freedom is under attack. We are bound by society on how we should live instead of God's blueprint for our lives. Our minds have been conformed by the world's standards, and we refuse to transform our minds and get back into position with the Lord. The Bible is the instructions, the combination of these two resources to "guide you into all truth" (John 16:13).

When we stand up for what's right and proclaim the Good News of the Gospel, we will be under attack. We are in a spiritual battle. We have a God who is faithful; He will not let you be tempted beyond what we can bear. Many times, we blame God for our weaknesses in being overcomers. But in reality, I find that I was not in the right position to overcome whatever the temptation was. I did not call on the Lord. I did not listen to the Holy Spirit and refused to surrender and submit to the leading of the Spirit.

We have to make time for God. It begins with prayer by asking God to help you make time. If we are to be victorious on this journey, we must take the right position. Praying without ceasing. Not only when things are going well. Paul said in the Word that he learned how to be abased and abound. See, most of the time, when things are going well, we tend to let our guard down and become comfortable and start relying on our minds and immediately forget about God. Nothing wrong with enjoying our seasons of abundance. But in the lean seasons, when we are trying to make ends meet, our health is not so good, family members are having struggles, we tend not to have the same excitement and drive when things are well. But remember the position of gratitude, thanksgiving, honor, and praise is due to God each day of our lives whether things are not as we want them to be.

We must always be aware of our spiritual struggles. Having a relationship with God daily keeps us in the position to be fully equipped to stand against the wiles of the enemy. There is a shield we must wear every day under the clothing that we wear to cover our flesh. We have instructions to put on the whole armor of God, to not only stand but to withstand against any attack of our body and soul.

I found out in storm that I needed God to give me the strength and courage to trust Him no matter how severe the storm. In that storm, I lost my position by yielding to my flesh. Even though I knew that God was with me, I struggled in my flesh for how I felt in my physical body. One thing I found out that I was not going to be victorious unless I became obedient to listen to the Holy Spirit who assured me that God was with me. My illness did not catch God by surprise. He is omnipotent. In my valley experience, God revealed himself. Sometimes, I wondered where God was. I knew Him, but because of a mind set in concentrating on the brokenness of my illness, trying to figure out the outcome, my days and nights were long. I began to understand the midnight hour experiences people talked about. I began to understand, no matter how saved, sanctified, you think you are, it's always tested when the storms are raging. I had to get in the right position to know He was there all the time. The words that were hidden in my heart came to life. Now I was totally surrendered to hear God's comfort through the Holy Spirit and His Son Jesus. I began to remember His promises; I began to listen to His loving kindness in the Spirit. He was making me stronger; He was molding me from the desperation of my spirit trying to figure when things will change. All things happen in God's timing, and we must trust Him. I had to ask His forgiveness for not trusting. Many distractions will come when you stay in position and alignment to God.

Shaped for Valley Experiences

One may ask, "What is a valley experience?" For those that don't know they are the lifetime experiences that allows us to look back and see the growth of our walk with the Lord. Valley experiences bring a sense of appreciation in not taking life for granted and appreciating that your today can change in an instant and you don't have time to waste. Every moment of life is precious, and it allows us not to complain but appreciate where you are in Christ. Sometimes we go unaware that we have a High Priest and an intercessor that pleads before God our case. When we are not trusting our intercessor, Jesus goes to the Father and pray for us and interpret what is truly in our hearts and mind. He understands our weaknesses. He understands our lack of faith in Him. We all can have different interpretations of the experiences we go through in life, and none will be the same. But my storms do not make me better than you; neither your storms make you better. It's how we come out of the storms. But the outcome of how we go through is a clear sign of what we believe, whom we trust, and how much we want to be victorious over our storms and trials in our life. I don't think anyone wants to go through anything if they don't have to. Donna Partow, author of the book, This Isn't the Life I Signed Up For, writes about finding hope and healing in the things we go through. You can't always control what happens to you, but you can choose how you will respond. No one signs up for challenges of life, but in the real world, tough times are inevitable. We know if God created a flawless world that always chooses to do what's right, there will be no problems. Everything, except man, in the universe obeys God. He gave man free will to choose between good and evil. Most of the times, we make the wrong decisions expecting good outcomes. You can't control what happens to you, but you can choose how you respond. I always envision myself on an island enjoying the sounds of the waves from the beach, feeling the breeze, and inhaling and basking in the beauty of that moment. Nothing wrong with that moment, but I am facing the realities of my choices to respond in a positive way and deal with it or to escape in a fantasy world of my own? The sooner I find hope and accept what I cannot change, then I embrace my healing process to know that with God, all things work for my good and all for His glory. We would rather bypass any storm or any trial and live a carefree life of no balances that may come our way. Our character is shaped by the determination and drive of our minds to first understand that we have no power to overcome anything in this life on our own strength unless it's in the Lord. The twenty-third psalm gives us a promise and assurance that we have a shepherd that watches over us, and there is no lack in us if we trust Him. He said we shall not want. Another assurance He tells us is "Though we walk through the shadows of death we shall not fear any evil for He is with us. He gives us comfort with His rod and staff." We enjoy the mountaintop experiences. Everything is beautiful on the top. Many times, we can see the top, and we avoid the valley. To get to the top, you must go through the valley. We must understand that the valley is a temporary place. It is a part of our lives. Sometimes we wonder why God allows these valley experiences in our lives. We think God is punishing us or trying to get our attention. I found out in my valley experiences how much God loves me and that He was working a miracle in my life and revealing Himself to me. We have to realize that when we are going through valley storms; it's not the end. God has set his timing for you to come out. Some may take longer because we will not yield to the love of God that He knows what's best for us to weather the storms in our life, and He has all the tools we need to be victorious. It's like cooking something, you set the timer for how many minutes or hours something should be done, and then it's done. And remember, you check it—you just don't look at it—and say it's done. So, whatever you are cooking has to go through a process—heat, cold, cooling period—for the final outcome to be beautiful and satisfactory to as you expected. So is God's timing.

In our valley storms, God's grace is with us, and His mercy will never fail us. I have been guilty in my valley storms of wanting a quick release from my storm. I ask God many questions, like Habakkuk, "How long, God? God, what did I do to deserve this suffering? Lord, where are You?" The one thing that kept me from not losing my mind when the enemy came in so many ways to discredit my mind with questions like "Where is God? How can He allow you to go through like this?" You know Him, and He is speaking to you. Just give up. But in my quiet times, I heard and felt the presence of the Lord through His Spirit, saying, "Trust Me. I will never leave you or forsake you." The devil's main attack mode is fear because the enemy begins to let you feel that you are alone. Don't give up in your valley experiences. In valley experiences, you have to remind yourself of what you know. In my experience, I had to hold fast to what I knew and speak life into my life with His Word. I had to remind myself that I am a child of God. I had to remember His promises. I had to remember that there is a purpose for my life. I had to remember to sing songs of praise and worship to bring comfort to my soul even when I did not feel like it. Patience was taught in my valley storm. It's okay to moan and cry out; I did. I realize how awesome God is because His eyes are always on us. I came out of my valley experience, stronger, better, wiser. Valley experiences are humbling, and it will always remind you not so much how much you endured but how you endured with God's love. And now you can be a blueprint for someone's life to help them reach out to God and know that they are more than conquerors. God does not leave us in the valley. He gives us mountaintop experiences to enjoy. Both experiences are testimonials of how great God is!

Moving from Your Past to Your Destiny

Moving on is one of the hardest things in life. Once we take the initial step, it will be the best decision you will be making toward your destiny. Letting go of the past and looking ahead to your destiny is a process that takes time, but the end result are awesome. You may ask yourself, "How do I let go? It hurts too bad. I am afraid." Isaiah 43:18–19 gave an example of God's people holding on tightly to the past that they missed the new thing God wanted to show them. We cannot change the past, but we certainly can change our future by embracing and letting go of the past. I find when I don't change my thought of the past, the enemy enforces his authority in my mind by keeping me bound to the past, but when I transform my mind to the promises and Word of God, my mind is renewed to trust God and let go. The beautiful thing about letting go is we step into a new creation with God. We are no longer bound by our past; we are forgiven and set free to begin again. When I am having struggles with letting go, I turn to God's

Word for strength and direction. Is the enemy going to continue to remind you of your past? Yes, that is his job to keep you separated from trusting God. Remember, he has no power unless you surrender it to him. "Cast all your care on God; God will sustain you, He will never let you be shaken" (Psalm 55:22). Moving requires changes. Changing from old habits, bad habits to adopting better habits that will help us grow. One of life's sayings is "what's done is done." With God, all things are possible if you only believe. What's gone is gone. One of life's lessons is always moving on. It's okay to look back and think of fond memories but keep moving forward. Moving does not mean you forget things. It just means you have accepted what happened and continue living. How we get to the part is easier said than done. We talked about something rather than discussing or how we can accomplish letting go of the past and moving forward to our destiny. Some things in our past are hurtful, we rather not even bring it up because it hurts, and when we share it with someone we confide in, it still doesn't seem to make the memory or the pain go away. But only you know if you have dealt with pains and hurts and you are no longer a prisoner to it and you have released it to God. We have scars from past experiences, but we have a God who says he has cast our sins as far as the east is from the west. Someone may say that sounds good. It is good because man cannot bring a peace in our souls that causes us to move forward forgetting those things that are behind and pressing as Paul said toward the mark our future and hope in Christ. People might say you need to get over it, but that is easier said than done. We may get into a heated discussion, trying to explain our pain and hurts, and this causes the wounds to be opened and the pain to be real all over again. Paul said, "Brethren, I count not myself to have apprehended, but this one thing I do, forgetting those things which are behind and reaching forth unto those things which are before, I press toward the mark for the prize of the high calling of God in Christ Jesus." We cannot change the past, and we certainly can't take it back. Things in our past hurt us and keeps us bound. God has our destiny ahead for us, but we must learn to let go of the old. Remember things are not always what they seem. The Israelites thought their lives were better in slavery. Our flesh will always keep us bound up. We must walk in the Spirit and allow God to heal and mend our broken heart in things we have kept hidden in our hearts, and we think no one knows. But God does know. He is so gracious and faithful that He said, "I cast your sins as far as the east is from the west." Instead of dwelling on how bad your past was, dwell on God's promises to you. The enemy will always try to remind you of your past failures. Tell the enemy, "So what! I am still here so I can start all over. Because my God is a forgiving God, merciful God.

There are so many things to be excited about, but we never seem to remember them when our mind-set is on the negative. You have new beginnings in Christ. He said, "Come unto me all that are heavy laden and I will give you rest. We need rest for our souls. We have been carrying our burdens too long. Have faith in God. We need faith to move from our past to our destiny. It begins with you having an attitude of a champion. Wanting to put on your armor the armor of God (Ephesians 6:10–18). Finally, be strong in the Lord and in his mighty power. "Put on the full armor of God that you may be able to stand against the wiles of the devil." God wants to teach us how to experience victory in spiritual combat. Although our armor and weapons are spiritual, it does not mean they are unreal or ineffective. "For though we walk in the flesh we do not war after the flesh" (2 Corinthians 10:3, 4) (for the weapons of our warfare are not carnal, but mighty through God to the pulling down of strongholds). Do a little each day to move forward from your fleshly thoughts to the spiritual realm. There will be obstacles in your way. Remember it's going to be a process, but you will win with the Lord. He fights for you. No weapon form against you will prosper as long as you keep your eyes on God. Sometimes fear will not allow us to let go. "But Jesus immediately said to them: 'Take courage! It is I. Don't be afraid'" (Matthew 14:2–31). Our destiny holds things we should be enjoying and letting go of. It's time to lay aside everything that is holding you back. To walk to your destiny, you must lay aside anything that you did not give up. Life is to be enjoyed. Jesus said He came to give us life and life more abundantly. Now that does not sound like a life of grief and sorrows, disappointments, failures. Don't look back at your failures. Stop spending your time dwelling on your past. Look to God. See through His eyes how He sees you. The world calls us losers when we are not walking according to their evils. God calls us conquerors—His child—when we become totally surrendered to Him and have accepted Him as our personal savior and Lord. Don't allow the enemy to rob you from moving from your past to your destiny. "Behold, I will do a new thing, now it shall spring forth, shall ye not know it? I will even make a way in the wilderness, and rivers in the dessert. You will see the change" (Isaiah 43:19). The story of Lot's wife is told in Genesis 19:2, "But Lot's wife looked back as she was following behind him, and she turned into a pillar of salt." She was looking back at her past. She received a warning. She was not willing to accept the warning. What she chose to value in her heart led her to sin, which led to her death. I am sure we have asked these questions, "What is my destiny? Why do I exist? Is there a reason or purpose for my life?" God has a plan for our happiness. If we want to rise to life's challenges and move to our destiny, knowing good and evil allows us to prove ourselves; it encourages us to study God's Word, to keep His commandments, and to build a relationship with Him that He desires from all of us. Allow Him to lead you out of your past to your destiny.

It's Too Hard

As I go about my daily task each day, I think about how many people live on the phrase "It's too hard." I think about so many conditions people have endured, gone through, and those that are living with the disabilities of some hardships that were not in their control. I would like to share this one story that will give you hope no matter what you face in life. On one of my many visits to the convalescent homes for the Outreach Ministries of U2 Can Share, I met this wonderful lady name Opal. I introduced myself to her, told her Jesus loves her. Her response was so heartwarming to the fact that she responded with such joy like she had an experience with Jesus. Opal had both of her legs amputated because of her diabetes. She never complained about her condition. Opal made friends with everyone. I looked forward to seeing Opal on my visit. She became a mother to me. Opal shared her wisdom and knowledge of God. Opal's health began to fail, and as I continue to visit and talk with her, she talked about her favorite song "His Anchor Holds." In my visits, we sang lots of spiritual songs.

While I was going through my storms, she encouraged me. When I left my visits with Opal, I was encouraged. I realize Opal was an angel by God sent to me. In spite of her illness, Opal's mind was sharp. She accepted her condition. She knew God loves her, and I believe it was God's love that kept her from saying "It's too hard." Opal wanted to go home, but God was not ready yet. He kept her here long enough to share His love with others, and she certainly touched my life. Opal went on home to be with the Lord where one day, I will see her again running around on her new legs, shouting, "Glory, glory to the most High God!"

"For I consider that our present sufferings are not worth comparing with the glory that will be revealed in us. (If you don't suffer you cannot reign with me)." (Romans 8:18)

The word "suffering" in our mind denotes gain, physical stress, emotional imbalance, distress. When we associate with the word "suffering" and its meaning, we think that our lives are going to be altered. In our mind, when things are balanced according to our humanistic comprehension, we define that as being happy, in control. When we think of suffering, we think of pain, a pain you feel when you lose a loved one or when someone is killed, an accident that caused paralysis and altered someone life. When we get bad news from the doctor of an incurable disease. A tornado devastating a country. A tsunami, an earthquake. Yes, there is great suffering taking place, emotionally and mentally. Any state of undergoing pain, distress, or hardship is defined in our minds as suffering. Anything unpleasant in our life, we associate it with suffering. We endure unpleasant things in life, a person gets cancer, a person copes with injustice being treated unfairly by a relative or the world, a person grieving a loss. We bear up under all these pressures, but in all this, it does not compare to the glory that will be revealed in us.

"For our light momentary troubles worketh for us far more exceeding and eternal weight of glory. Is the way we endure with faith. We forget the prize of eternal life. Life is short and eternity is forever (refer 1:3-9). (2 Corinthians 4:17)

Fully Loaded

There are giants in our lives that cripple us and keep us bound if we don't release our doubts and fears. The giants in our lives must be conquered. We have a great defender who is Jesus. We build giants of fear, doubt, self-worth, intimidation, lack of confidence, self-esteem, loneliness, abandonment, betrayal, rejection, abuse. All those giants live within us. We carry them around daily. There is a station of help; call God. He is our present help in the time of trouble. "God is our refuge and strength, a very present help in trouble" (Psalm 46:1). We live in fearful times. God is ever present in times like these. He is available to you. He is continually at our sides, speaking to us and guiding us. And he's made this possible by giving us His Holy Spirit, to abide in us. But, I really doubt that we understand this fully. We envision God is too busy for my problems, and the Holy Spirit only abides with the religious. In His Word, He said, "I leave you a gift, the Comforter" (John 14:16). "And I will ask the Father, and he will give you another advocate (the Holy Spirit) to help you and be with you forever."

We are great imitators of masking our giants; until we build up, the greatest enemy of our soul is fear. The devil uses his greatest weapon against the believers, fear. The world accepts us with these giants because the world operates in the temporal and what can be visible or seen. I call it a Band-Aid approach. Cover it up until it peels and smells, but it is not healed. Failure is not an acceptable description of overcoming fears in our lives. We must be overcomers of whatever holds or cripples or holds us hostage for any period of time. Sin takes us farther than we want to go and keeps us longer than we want to stay. We must be conquerors. God helped me through some rough periods of my life. He thought me to be an overcomer. Through a personal relationship with Him, I learned that He loves me. He understands what I am going through. He reveals Himself by extending His grace and mercy. He reveals Himself in my weakness. He was strong. He provided everything I needed. He taught me to fellowship with Him. I was pregnant at a young age and thought my life was over, not because I was pregnant but because I did not know how to cope. I had goals and dreams of accomplishing things. I was a dreamer. Things happen in all of our lives, and it is not all for bad. There are no mistakes with God. He understands that our human mind will make mistakes. What He wants us to understand that there is no condemnation (Romans 8:1) for those who belong to Christ Jesus, who walk not after the flesh, but after the Spirit. So, in the flesh, we wrestle, but in the Spirit with are free. There was a determination in me that wanted more than just the wrong decision I had made. I had a beautiful girl. I know there was a future for me and my family. I had many dreams and desires, but I was not fully loaded. I was partially loaded. That means I allowed many other things to penetrate my armor and kept me in worry, anxiety, depression, frustration, defeat. I knew within that the things will eventually destroy my character and will and God's plans. Back home in my homeland, Panama, I was a Catholic, not by choice, but there was a curious side of me that knew that Christianity was a better life than living tossed and driven by my own decision-making mechanism that was not leading me in the right direction; my past needed to be released to know my destination. I needed more. Predominantly, that was the religion back then. I am sure there were small groups of other faiths, meeting in small places. I knew of God, but I did not know God like I know Him today. There are journeys in our lives that bring us from different parts of life, some pleasant, some unpleasant. But whatever journey you find yourself on, the main ingredient to victorious living is having a relationship with God.

I attend the Catholic Church but never carried a Bible. After all, the priest was our intercessor, and there was no need for me to know truth. My mother held prayer meetings at the house, and as little children, we had to attend. We did not participate, but I paid attention and knew they were worshipping God in their way, so I guess some of it rubbed off on me because now I am saved and fully loaded for God. Each day, I praise God that being fully loaded helps me to deal with my everyday struggles and keeps me in His presence for my daily nourishments. Fully loaded keeps me humble before God, always seeking His guidance against the wiles of the enemy and the direction to stay focused in equipping the saints and a vessel for the Lord in the world, always having my weaponry of warfare ready for battle. We should take a daily inventory of our equipment. Are we running low on love, forgiveness, hope, encouragement? I constantly stay in prayer every day seeking all that I need to be a survivor on this journey.

Finish Strong

I returned and saw under the sun that the
race is not to the swift, nor the battle to
the strong, neither yet bread to the wise,
nor yet riches to men of understanding, nor yet favour to men of skill; but
time and chance happeneth to them all.
(Ecclesiastes 9:11)

We must finish the race strong. Paul mentioned in
Philippians 3:14 that he presses toward the mark for the
prize of the high calling of God in Christ Jesus. We must
pursue as Paul did for the goal of the prize promised by
God. We must fight a good fight and finish the course and
keep the faith. There is a treasure laid up for those that
will endure to the end. A crown of righteousness. There
is a conditioning period of our lives that we go through.
This conditioning period shapes us for the journeys ahead
of our lives. It may seem hard what you are going through,
but in the flesh, we always see things differently because

we are relying on our ability to bring things to pass and to get the results we want. In the race, we know that there is a finish line. But before the race, we have to come to the starting line. By the time we are at the starting line, we have conditioned our minds that we want to win the race. In our minds, we always measure someone's self-worth by their accomplishments. But your measure is to the Lord. But in reality, our mind is set on twirling with thoughts of our conditioning. Did we do all in our power to be able to make it out of the starting position to get the results we want to win.

Many have come to the starting position and turned back. The story of the lost son. "There was a man who had two sons. The younger said to his father, 'Father, give me my share of the estate.' So, he divided his property between them. Not long after that, the younger son got together all he had, set off for a distant country, and there he squandered his wealth in wild living. After he had spent everything, there was a severe famine in that whole country, and he began to be in need. So he went and hired himself out to a citizen of that country who send him to his field of pigs" (Luke 15:11–16). Remember all believers as prodigals who don't always turn back to God. In order for us to succeed; we must finish strong. It's not how you start; it's how you finish. The race is not given to the swift but to the one that endures to the end. First, we must recognize our circumstances. The prodigal son found out that we can meet God in any place at any time in our circumstances. It's amazing how our circumstances can give us a new perspective on our lives. Some of us have to hit rock bottom to be able to see clearly the things we do without God. Then the prodigal son had a conviction: "when he finally came to his senses, he said to himself, 'At home even the servants have food enough to spare and here I am dying of hunger!'" Have you ever found yourself in these conditions? He repented. He was not too proud to admit that he made a mistake and needed help. We have to deal with our sins. We must confess, not before man but to God. Our prayer as the prodigal son goes, "I am no longer worthy to be called your son; make me like one of your hired men." We must have godly sorrow. After all, He is not asking you to explain the story; He knows the story. Our prayers are to deny self, recognize our unworthiness, and turn back to God. Don't skip the steps to true repentance. Don't be insincere about confessing to God that you messed up. He honors true repentance.

Living a Victorious Life in Christ

And this is the victory that has overcome
the world—our faith. (1 John 5:4)

Today we have a million excuses for not living a victorious life, but unfortunately none of them will cut it as long as God is on the throne as an empowering force. The list of excuses we have can be very long or maybe just one that keeps us bound and not free. We allow the enemy to define our shortcomings from victory into defeats. We are not educated; we are not up to the standards of whatever our attainments may be. I come to let you know God says you can be victorious and that you are more than a conqueror if you trust Him and not lean to your own understanding. It's a good place to begin by casting all your care upon Him.

"Faith is the substance of things hope for and the evidence of things not seen" (Hebrews 11:1). We have to have audacious hope in the things that are rooted. Christ is the perfect example of things rooted. He displayed this hope on the cross at Calvary. No, it was not an easy journey but a victorious outcome, His death, burial, and resurrection. You can persevere under pressures of this world by totally surrendering to God and allowing Him to be Lord of your life. Attitudes of courage and faith need to be developed every day by spending time in prayer and meditation before God. The faster you realize that you are the vessel and not the source of the solution, the better you will be—now you can partner with God. God has a plan for your life. Jeremiah 29:11 tells us that He knows the plans He has for you. It is a blessing that God has you on His mind. He is always there to help you as you call on Him and spend time with Him seeking His wisdom and knowledge concerning your life. The plans He has is for your good, not disaster, and all that He be glorified through you. You are an epistle that the world needs to see how to live in victory not defeat. We need to transform our minds each day from disasters to victories. You must speak life. Proverbs 18:21 says the tongue has the power of life and death, and those who love by it will eat its fruits. What comes out of the mouth proceeds from the heart, and this defiles you. Luke 6:45 says, "A good person out of the good treasure of his heart produces good, and the evil treasures produces evil, for out of the abundance of the heart his mouth speaks. So we must overcome the negative thoughts and speak life in our spirit into existence. Words have power! Our prayers should sound like this: Lord, enlighten what's dark in me, strengthen what's weak in me, mend what's broken in me, bind what's bruised in me, heal what's sick in me, and lastly, receive whatever peace and love has died in me so I can begin to look up to you for my healing to live a victorious life.

Fears cripple us. Doubts surround us. These things need to be shattered in order for us to have victorious breakthroughs. It is not easy. We deal with fears and doubts every day. The opposite of faith is unbelief, not doubt. The emotions of worry, doubt, and fear take away all the joy from your life, but if you face these giants, you will overcome it with the help of the Lord. Joyce Myers speaks on how to defeat your doubts and fears. You have to feed your faith. You are lacking nourishment. If you don't take in the proper nourishment, it causes you to make poor choices, which make life difficult and not victorious. Stop wishing and take action; take control of your emotions. Remember, doubt and fear will always interrupt faith if you give it power. Nothing comes into existence in us until we give it power, and that is done in the power of your words. Speak life! Fight back! God is not expecting perfection from us. He is working in our lives through our faith in Him. Be determined to speak life into your life. Get up each day determined that something good is going to happen for me today; then expect it. The devil will interrupt your mind and flood your mind immediately with doubt and fear. Romans 10:17 tells us how "faith comes by hearing, and hearing by the Word of God." The key is the Word of God; that's the reason God tells us to hide the Word in our hearts that we might not sin against Him. At the attacks of the enemy in your mind, you can pull up the Word that is hidden in your heart and use it as your weaponry to respond to the attacks of the enemy that you are more than a conqueror and no weapon used against you shall prosper. God's Word is your medicine and the food we need for our soul to live a victorious life. Talk about what God has done for you. Talk about the storms He has brought you through. Talk about God's healing and deliverance in your life. Don't give energy to doubt or fears. To be victorious, you must feed your faith. In the book of Luke, when Jesus was in the wilderness, the devil came to tempt Him. When the devil spoke to Him, Jesus responded, "It is written . . . " and quoted the Word of God. He used the Word as a weapon to overcome the lies of the enemy. We must not neglect the necessary mental and physical preparation it takes each day to live a victorious life. You must present your bodies as a living sacrifice, holy and acceptable, which is your reasonable service to God. We must cast down everything outside of the Cross. It is through and in the Cross that we will have victory!

Physical preparation is necessary also. If you are tired all the time, you are not ready for the battle. The enemy attacks a weak vessel that is not in Christ. Trust God, no matter what you are feeling and exercise your faith. It is impossible to live in victory without a victorious concept. If you are defeated in your thoughts with negative thoughts of failure, then you will never win. But if you set your mind on victories and being a conqueror, you will always win the battle. Remember something or someone will always steal your joy if you allow it, but we need the atmosphere of joy in the midst of our circumstances and trials. Joy brings strength, and sadness weakens your immune system. Think the way God thinks (1 Corinthians 2:9). Develop a vision of victory (Isaiah 43:19). Make a plan (Proverbs 16:3). Declare the truth over your situation until the facts line up with His Word (Isaiah 45:21). Stand strong during adversity (Ecclesiastes 9:11).

Begin today to have the mind of Christ. The Bible says, "The path of the righteous grows brighter and brighter and brighter." Think increase. think big, think expansive (notice that is not a typo). Many associate the word "expensive" with victorious living with the wealth and materials. Be determined to live each day filled with faith and expectancy that God is helping you live a victorious life. Commit to the Lord. Declare the truth over every situation in your life until the facts line up with His Word!

Know Your Identity

For you have been bought with a
price: Therefore glorify God in your
body, and in your spirit, which are
God's. (1 Corinthians 6:20)

This is a personal question we must each ask ourselves, and the only answer comes from the Word of God in reference to man's identity. The Bible tells us, "Therefore, if anyone is in Christ, he is a new creation. The old has passed away; behold, the new has come. We are a chosen race, a royal priesthood, a holy nation, a people for his own possession, that you may proclaim the excellences of Him who called you out of darkness into His marvelous light." So we identify that we are not a creation of darkness but of light. For in Christ, we are all sons and daughters through faith.

We do not identify with the world because we are in it but not of it. God identified us as His people who are called by His name who would humble themselves, seek His face, pray, and turn from their wicked ways, then we will hear from heaven, and He will heal our land. We hear the voices of the world that says, "Why are all these things happening? Why are bad things happening to good people? Why so much suffering in the world and God does not intervene?" There is a separation between the world and God's people. He has given all of us an identity, but we must choose whose side we are on: the ruler of this world, the enemy, or the one who created the world and the enemy to know that everyone born of God does not keep on sinning, but he who was born of God protects him, and the evil one does not touch him. Our citizenship is in heaven; from it we await a savior, the Lord Jesus Christ. The world has given up their citizenship to the world and forfeiting their inheritance eternal life.

Our identity is to boldly accept that we have been crucified with Christ. We have accepted Him as our Lord of our lives, and we are sold out for Christ and, having been set free from sin, have become slaves to righteousness. We are set free from the world's identity by serving God and walking in His ways. Therefore, we do not accept the condemnation of the world, for we are in Christ. For the law of the spirit of life has set us free in Christ Jesus from the law of sin and death. For God has done what the law, weakened by the flesh, could not do. By sending His only-begotten Son in the likeness of sinful flesh and for sin, he condemned sin in the flesh in order that the righteous requirement of the law might be fulfilled in us, who walk not according to the flesh but according to the Spirit. For those who live according to the flesh set their minds on things of the flesh, but those who live according to the Spirit set their minds on the things of the Spirit. We have been transferred to a different domain, the one from darkness into the kingdom of God's beloved Son Jesus.

Should we continue in sin? God forbid. The wages of sin is death. The world offers death and destruction. The world offers things that will leave you empty and abandoned; these things wage war against your soul. Many have not died and their lives are not hidden in Christ. They are exposed and blinded by the ways of the world. The world today grieves the Holy Spirit of God; by being born, they were sealed for the day of redemption. They have sold their identity to the devil. God is a merciful God and loving in all His ways that He extends His promises to all that will surrender to Him.

We live in a world where we are not sure of our identity. Depending on how we feel and what issues are being discussed, we tend to be distracted and easily swayed away from what we know spiritually is right according to God's Word. Going back to the scripture, "If my people," there was our identity, not in question, if we believe that we are His people. Before I came to the Lord did not now my identity. I knew I was part of a family that consisted of a father, mother, and seven siblings. We were raised to be respectful, to have love for one another. There were moral values that were implanted in our hearts growing up. As time went by, after childhood into adulthood, I was curious of what I wanted to do with my life, so I identified with looking at other people's accomplishments and aspiring to become like them in some way to be recognized or identified or make a mark in life as to who I am. I became curious about being an airline stewardess; after all, I would be recognized in helping people and meeting people all over the world. Doing more research, I discovered that the identity dream was fading quickly because I heard of all airplane crashes and death. That identity faded in the wind. I was very good at sports: softball, track, tennis, and because of my accomplishments and success, I soon clung to that identity. I would be a great athlete and recognized. Because of injuries, that identity faded out into the horizon. I was introduced to Jesus by my sister-in-law Pat who invited me to her church. I watched the people sing and praise God. I saw the joy that it brought to them. I felt something tugging at my heart. I felt they were identifying with God who gave them a purpose and a reason to honor Him. I became curious. At that point in time of my life, I really did not know God. I knew of Him but never had a personal relationship with Him. Because of how I felt on that day at church, when I went home getting ready for bed in the still of the night, God called my name as plain as if I said it. His words were "I love you, daughter, and I am here for you." I said, "Yes, Lord," with tears streaming down. I want to know more about you and began reading the Word, and God gave me peace and direction of who I was and the purpose of my life. Now I know my identity and have been running for Jesus a long time and I am not tired! God is the perfect model of my identity. They are many things that will challenge our identity. We must confirm it by the Word and stand on its affirmations that we are wonderfully and fearfully made by him. Our identity cannot be split. To be double-minded is an enmity against God. Know your identity, and you will be set free. I went many places and looked at too many things to find my identity all along was already designed, prepared for me by the Father. His love drew me close to who I am and what I was set apart to do. Many people are still struggling with things to identify themselves with and to. They become victims of this society. This world has compartments of where you fit. God does not. You have a place that is waiting for you; it's prepared for you, but you have to take ownership of your identity to receive your inheritance. Step out on faith. God identified Himself to us. "For God so loved the world that He gave His only begotten Son that whosoever believe on Him should not perish but have everlasting life" (John 3:16). There is no life in the world; God promises everlasting life. He is a God that cannot lie. He proved that greater love had no man that he laid down His life for us. Don't continue to allow the enemy to steal your identify. Identify that the devil is the enemy of your soul and he speaks lies; he is the father of lies and speak the Word at him. "Satan, I plead the blood of Jesus against you. You are already defeated, and you have no victory or authority over me." We are living in a world that need emotional healing, and we should be the epistle that the world can identify that there is hope in Christ no matter how bad things may seem or what they have done and where they find themselves at the time; if they will identify themselves as God's people, giving up the life of sin and turning back to a God whose love is unconditional and intentional for the saving of their soul.

Prayer: God, I confess all my sins to you and ask you to release me from the bondage of sin and receive me into your unconditional love for me that I can boldly take a stand on my identity that's in You. Amen.

Spiritual Wellness

We can never use the measurements of our physical well-being by how we feel physically. The question, "how do I feel spiritually?" determines my next move of how I operate starting with my emotions. Feeling well is a measurement of discerning how we would function every day. Our balance of how we operate daily is measured by how we feel physically, how much energy we will give to our daily task, and how long we will engage in it. We define spiritual wellness as everything is operating the way we see and feel it. It revolves on some specific things happening at points and times. Wellness is defined as having possessions, money, who we know, what social group we belong to, where we live, what accomplishments we have attained. Physically wellness begins in our minds. As I rise in the morning, my mind shifts to how I am feeling in my body. I noticed that when I pray before getting up that when I pray the daily prayer "Our Father, which art in heaven . . .," it releases my mind from concentrating on my condition, and it shifts my mind by allowing God to have full control of my mind and how I will operate in that day. So, my day begins with an assurance that God is with me. He has already blessed my day, and even though I might feel some light afflictions, whether it be sickness, something you are dealing with, disappointments, unforgiveness, jealousy, envy, relationships marriage, parenting, children, God is the solution for spiritual wellness in all areas of your life.

Spiritual wellness is a process that helps us find meaning in life. We can use meditation, affirmations, prayer to keep us spiritually and physically well. How do you treat yourself? Because of our busy schedules and taking care of everyone but ourselves, we neglect the wellness of our soul and find ourselves out of alignment. Our thoughts need to be arrested back to good thoughts. We have to get our thoughts and emotions aligned with love, peace, compassion, knowledge, joy, freedom, appreciation, gratitude, forgiveness, passion, happiness, positive thinking and beliefs, hope. We must be a sponge to absorb the things of God that brings us back into alignment with who we are and how we should operate in the war we are in. Our spiritual wellness affects the lives that are around us. Someone is watching how you operate every day by your actions and the language of your body and the words that come out of your wellness.

Our perfect example comes from God, His character and His unfailing love for us. Our spiritual condition is important for the journey we are in. The journey is to make heaven our home. We have a destination that is mapped out for us, and we have been given a roadmap to get there. The journey begins with you being equipped. We are fighting spiritual wars. We have to take a stand against evil forces. If you don't believe you are in a battle, take a check of your daily life. Even though we don't see our attacker, he is real; he is the enemy of your soul that wants to keep you bound and not well for the battle. We feel the forces of his impact every day. Regardless of our opinion, there is a battle going on. You must take the necessary steps each day to nurture and encourage your spiritual wellness. I shared earlier in previous chapters of my valley experience. I was not physically well. Emotionally I had become spiritually weak and that took me to the pit of not been well spiritually. This happened because I was not nurturing my spirit in the things of God but concentrated on the physical pain that I was in. It was not until I realize in the Spirit that I was in a warfare and I had allowed myself to be weakened by the forces of my flesh. I began to mind the things of the flesh and not of the Spirit. God, in his intentional love, brought deliverance to my condition by reminding me if I nurture the spirit man, I would find healing and deliverance from my condition, if I will reinforce what I already knew. His Word was healing power for my soul. By His stripes, I am healed that He was wounded for our transgressions and bruised for our iniquities: the chastisement of our peace was upon him, and with his stripes we are healed. I remembered a cheerful heart is good medicine, but a crushed spirit dries up the bones. God wanted me spiritually well. Through that experience, I can testify that if it had not been for God on my side, where would I be? I strive each day to be an encourager and motivation by my testimony that we serve an awesome God who knows every infirmity. Hebrews 4:15 tells us that the High Priest of ours understands our weaknesses, for He faced all of the same things . . . with the feelings of our infirmities, but was in all points tempted like as we are, yet without sin. God's Word is medicine for our soul; it's a prescription for life. Take it till it's all gone. The expiration date is Judgment Day. Would you be there? "Just as people are destined to die once and after that comes judgment" (Hebrews 9:27). Unless the second coming of Jesus Christ occurs in your lifetime, you personally cannot be exempted from death. In all exemptions, the Bible gives two. One was Enoch (Genesis 5:23–24) and Elijah (2 Kings 2:1, 11). Quote: If you escape death only to face judgment, the stale cliché might find fresh meaning: "out of the frying pan into the fire." Spiritually well means you are ready for what's stored up for you in glory.

About the Author

Evangelist Sandra Green

Evangelist Sandra Green is a born-again Christian. God gave her a vision of a ministry called U2 Can Share Outreach Ministries. This vision has been on the move every day for God in her everyday living. She has a great passion for the wellness of God's people. The Word of God is used as her weapon of warfare against principalities, wickedness, and evil in this world today. She gives hope to the lost and assurance that God's love is the ultimate and only love that will sustain us. She promotes the gospel and evangelizes the Word. The Word of God is her foundation she stands on, and her faith is displayed by her testimonies of what God will and can do. The ministry is available to pray with others, help feed the needy, and bring the light of salvation to the world through Christ.

Spiritual wellness is one of her many passions, and living a victorious life for Christ is what she promotes in this ministry. She is a great listener, not only to people's lives, but also to the Spirit of God's instructions to apply the wisdom to help others and herself be an overcomer in whatever struggles we face with the help of God. She is a mother of four, grandmother of thirteen, and great-grandmother of five. She believes in the principle of divine inspiration with a victorious attitude.

This book, *Fully Loaded*, is an inspirational book that will equip and empower us to be more than conquerors in our daily struggles in life.

CPSIA information can be obtained
at www.ICGtesting.com
Printed in the USA
FSOW01n0606200117
29797FS